OBAMA MENTUM
(An Anthology of Transformational Poetry)
POEMS

Kraftgriots

Also in the series (POETRY)

OBAMA MENTUM
(An Anthology of Transformational Poetry)

POEMS

Edited by
Abdul-Rasheed Na'Allah

kraftgriots

Published by

Kraft Books Limited
6A Polytechnic Road, Sango, Ibadan
Box 22084, University of Ibadan Post Office
Ibadan, Oyo State, Nigeria
℗ +234 (0)803 348 2474, +234 (0)805 129 1191
E-mail: kraftbooks@yahoo.com;
kraftbookslimited@gmail.com
Website: www.kraftbookslimited.com

First published 2016

ISBN 978–978–918–361–6

= KRAFTGRIOTS =
(A literary imprint of Kraft Books Limited)

First printing, February 2016

For my beloved father, Ahmad Alabi Na'Allah, poet and scholar!

Acknowledgements

First, gratitude is to the Almighty God, for the opportunity to yet again present a collective forum to the world. I am obviously taking a clue from my first presentation in 1998 of *Ogoni's Agonies* (AWP) where, in poetry and in critical essays, poets and scholars gathered to respond to the brutal murder of a Nobel Peace Prize nominee, Ken Saro-Wiwa, who was championing the cause of his mercilessly wounded people of the oil-rich Nigerian Delta. This current effort is different, almost opposite, since it is in a more joyous cause. The emergence of a transformational world leader in the person of Barack Obama, elected in November 2008 (precisely one decade after *Ogoni's Agonies*) in which hope and spirit of fairness, multilateralism, and cultural plurality are rekindled. I want to thank Becky Clarke from whom the support and zeal to make this anthology a certainty were firm.

Erica Reckamp, my editorial coordinator, without whose hard work this anthology might not have become a reality. Also to poets from across the world who served as jury in the selection of the poems that made it to this book. I am sure they will be proud of the final product of their labor. Finally to all those writers who responded to my "Call for Poems" to celebrate the emergence of Barack Obama as President of the United States. I am convinced that this work has helped us all to capture permanently in words, motion and performance, the world's very dramatic response to the election of this leader of the pluralistic world.

It is my hope that this poetry will contribute to the world's hope in a true rebirth of the concept of responsible and inspirational leadership in the twenty-first century!

Abdul-Rasheed Na'Allah
November 2009, Ilorin, Nigeria

Foreword

November 4, 2008, the night that Barak Obama was elected president, may come to be remembered not just as a significant historical event but a poetic moment, one that demanded response in verse rather than prose. From the tears flowing from Jesse Jackson's face in Grant Park, Chicago, to the ululations of women in Kisumu, Kenya and Jakarta, Indonesia, it was as if a dam of pent up emotions had been opened. The election of the first black president of the United States was so momentous that it seemed to beg for the kind of affective response that only poetry can enable. Poetry seemed to brush aside the language of politics. But, if as Niyi Osundare's poem, "Obama," which opens this collection rightly wonders, if the election of Obama was an "unusual melody" riding the music of his name, "How can its poetry Survive the prose of platitudinous politics?" Obama's moment seemed to put poetics and politics, even poetry and prose, into an unusual encounter. It was as if Obama was heralding a moment that had hence been better left unspoken, an event that had not, until then, found expression in language. At least this is how the Obama moment seemed to Derek Walcott whose poem "Forty Acres" was published in the *Times of London* on November 5, 2008.

> Out of the turmoil emerges one emblem, an engraving —
> a young Negro at dawn in straw hat and overalls,
> an emblem of impossible prophecy, a crowd
> dividing like the furrow which a mule has ploughed,
> parting for their president:

The day after Walcott's poem appeared, Obama was seen in the streets of Chicago carrying a copy of Walcott's *Collected Poems*. On seeing this picture—of the president waving the banner of the poet—some commentators were left with a few questions:

Did Obama aspire to be the poet president, too? Did he perhaps reckon that when history was being made against both the consciousness of history and the demands of an unjust past that it could only be expressed in an elevated language? This is perhaps what Elizabeth Alexander assumed when she wrote "Praise Song for the Day," a poem commissioned to commemorate Obama's first inauguration on January, 2009.

> We encounter each other in words, words
> spiny or smooth, whispered or declaimed,
> words to consider, reconsider.

We can add to this repertoire of Obama poems, the poems collected in *Obama Mentum*, all written in response to a call made by Abdul-Rasheed Na'Allah to poets around the world to respond to the Obama moment. These poems stand out because of their recognition of how poetry continues to be asked to be the handmaiden of events that are so momentous that they cannot be represented in ordinary language. These are poems driven by the energy of history as an irruption, a drive noted in the first verse of Niyi Osundare's poem:

> The hand that once picked cotton
> Has grabbed the crown
> The whip which once cut like hateful blade
> Has become a wand in the hand of the slave.

Time may have passed since that night on November 4, 2008 when Obama was first elected president, and perhaps the monumentality of the event has been tampered by time; still, reading this collection is a constant reminder of the tensions that went into the making of the black president as an icon.

In reading the collection I was struck by a number of issues revolving around the figure of Obama as person, an icon, and an event. For one, the poets are concerned about the meaning of Obama: Is he a sign of the future or a reminder of the past? If

8

Obama's irruption into the site of history appears to some poets as the signification of new hope, he is also a reminder of the historical repressed. So in temporal terms, Obama looks both forwards and backwards, reminding us of the utopian possibilities embodied by the skinny man with an African and Muslim name, but also marking the time before—the violence of slavery and colonialism, Jim Crow—and the difficult match toward freedom.

Another dimension in this collection concerns the different historical contexts in which Obama is imagined. As a mnemonic figure he takes the poets back to their own beginnings, reminding us that only recently the very idea of a black American president was unimaginable. A large number of poems in this collection are thus concerned with the difference that day in November 2008 would make in the narrative of history. The Obama moment is hence celebrated as a caesura—as break and connection with the past and an interruption. Osundare's poem captures this break vividly

> Intimations of changing waters
> Northern trees surprised the season
> With the magic of a winter blossom

Finally, it is important to note the diversity of voices collected in *Obama Mentum*. There are established poets in this collection, but also new voices. I was especially struck by the presence of people who had not written poems before the Obama moment, a testament to the power of the event to generate language. *Obama Mentum* is an invitation to rethink the role of the poetic voice as testimony and prophesy.

Simon Gikandi
Robert Schirmer Professor
Princeton University

Contents

I.
New Hope

Obama

"... a nation cannot prosper long when it favours only the prosperous"

"The world has changed...."

I

The hand that once picked cotton
Has grabbed the crown
The whip which once cut like hateful blade
Has become a wand in the hand of the slave

The path to this moment was snared with thorns
The climb stiff, unspeakably narrow
But History waited, as always,
With a riddle at the bend in the road

Cauterized with his colour
Crucified with his creed
Taunted with his tribe
A skinny neophyte with an African name

Sent Hope on an unprecedented errand;
The world rose in assent
The sea was never the same again.
A rainbow union unchained the sky

Engulfing the monochromatic mantra
Of skin-merchants; plural illuminations
Ascended, giving name and nous
To all that was dark and cruelly hidden

New dawn, new dusk
New possibilities, new visions

A common language outspeaks
The shibboleths of bygone days

A new truth is coming to Power,
Supple, cant-free, intelligently fluent:
Compassion is not out of fashion
Difference is no disadvantage

A palace, black-built, white-named,
Has encountered the rainbow touch;
No longer through the back door:
The people are more permanent than the paint

So much to build, so much to re-build
In a world laid waste by war and want
And the cannibal greed of the corporate cartel,
A season held hostage by hate and fear

Yes, We Can
The world sings from pole to pole
Yes, We Can
The future says Amen to the audacity of Change

The Dream . . . fleshed forth, at last;
The prophecy came to pass.
I can see Atlanta's uncrowned King
Smiling cautiously in his resting place

II

O-b-a-m-a

Destiny whispered that name into
History's ears. History gave it to the wind
There are no leaves on our tree

Not stirred by its breeze
No tongue in our world
Untouched by its magic accent

From Kisumu to Kingston
From Melbourne to Mumbai
Wherever every dawn

The sun opens up the eye of day
It is the crystal drop on the crown
Of the morning grass.

The passing cloud heard that name
And discharged its rain
Drought-time over, the season roused

The earth to wheat and wisdom
The mountain heard it and shifted a foot
Rivers gambolled uphill, unstoppably keen

Grain after grain after grain
Beach sands glittered into gold
The galloping tide arrived with

Intimations of changing waters
Northern trees surprised the season
With the magic of a winter blossom

An unusual melody rides the music
Of this name. How can its poetry
Survive the prose of platitudinous politics?

This colossus

Omofolabo Ajayi

Hearken!
Hope to haves, have-not-will-haves,
Have had, still haves, more to haves
Oppressed, repressed, stressed or not
Link hands of power to becoming
A new Colossus has come amongst us

This new Colossus is not one
Giant of classic statuesque.
It is a gentle breath of air
Awakening all from forty
Dream years and struggles
To Mountain Reality in sight.
This Colossus is momentous.

This Colossus no longer is
Just a lighted torch held aloft
A lady's hand pointing the way.
This torch lights from grounds
Up, hoisted from ancient shoulders
Sets ablaze zillion embers to action.
Together they travel the distance

This torch of the Colossus is one
Giant composite medley of masses
A tidal wave guiding an adrift
Ship to shores of safety 'n sanity.
Welcome aboard, pick up the paddle
Mind the sand dunes; slag not.
This journey is an uncharted phase.

The times are here, again

Mdika Nick Tembo

Cynics and doubting Thomases
have seen it all
but remain silent
wishing
they'd not shut you up.

Their miserly dreams
and infected handshakes
shudder
at the thought of new dawns
hugging the American people.

After 221 years of denial
and being hollered at
that America will never change,
unity
seemed a grave away.

Today,
a resilient American spirit
is enough to tell us,
that with fortitude
all things are possible.

Obama's global victory

Oritseweyinmi
Oghanrandukun Olomu

Back load of lies stood bold like turtle's shell
Upon our backs, romancing us with blames,
Our faces, bare like kings in sorry cells.
Raw hammer strikes cracked our joys and frames.
We hid in shells, unmoved by tongues that jeered;
Like turtles, we carried our weight of load
Away from fun, where no jolly thing neared,
Where anger ruled and angry passions rode.
Lo! Beauty smiles upon our lives with joy,
Removing sad tales of a foregone time.
Lo! Riches tames our hearts from much annoy;
Deploying our sweet souls to beauteous clime.
Lo! Success joys at the root of our lives;
As Obama fills our lives with sweet jives.

Winner

Megan Webster

(2008 presidential election)

We stand among millions
share the same lover.
We stand shoulder to shoulder
in a crowd whose tail runs past our land's borders.
Tears spark our faces.
Tears of love for the winner
our new lover who
swears he loves us back.
Tears of promise to tighten belts
grow up & face the mess
we're embroiled in.
Shoulder to shoulder we hail our winner.
"You did it America," he gleams
his smile overflowing
the world's wide screen.
Our tears crest with trust.
He waves — our eyes blaze.
"Hope in the face of adversity," he cries.

"Hope!" we shout, "Hope!"

The man who came out of the dark

Norbert Krapf

There was a man
who came out of the dark
but brought with him
the light so we could see.
This was a light he saw
deep in all of us and he
was able to give it a name,
more names than one.

The name of the light
that the man who came
from out of the dark
saw in each one of us
he sometimes called
you, sometimes *us*,
sometimes elevated
to the simple *we*.

This man who came
out of the dark but
could see the light
in all of us was part
black, part white,
part me, part you,
part of all of us.

His greatest gift
was the gift of the word,
the right word that came
from beyond and inside him
and all of his people,
but also from inside us.

This word he gave to us
came from both sides
of himself and all sides
of ourselves. He knew
how to draw on the words
he inherited as someone
who loves the land
and the language of
the people, his and ours,
the language of our place
and its many peoples.

The man who came
from out of the dark
but saw the light in us
asked for the right
to speak to and for us
and we gave it to him

and he calls us to come
together to hear the word
that comes from beyond
and within us, is ours
to hear and re-shape
with our tongues to
share with the world.

This is the day
that The Word
became President
and came back
to live in the House
that is both Black
and White. This is
the day that the man
who came out of the dark

came to live in the white
light of the house that
black slaves once built
so that The Word could
one day come home.

Monument

Erica Reckamp

slowing on the gravel

passing cars
can't blame him for stopping

the stark dark of the leafless tree
and the water
still
moving
trickling
running

from the quiet of our car
we can hear the crackle of the branches
as they stretch up
popping out
of the sky snow
blur

father lets in a howl of voices
as he opens the door
leans in for a sip of coffee
two hours cold

then out again
camera slung over his shoulder
bent on capture

haze breaks
the white begins to glow:

bring out the best in us
bring out the best

the whisper of wind through glass:

bring out the best
bring out the best in us

my backseat breath
halos the tree

bring out the best
bring out the best in us

if this dark, stark tree
was a sinewy man
reaching up, stretching
my father would plead:

bring out the best
bring out the best in us

reluctant
firing looks back
my father returns in a slow trek

it was something to see

we in the back
can't blame him for stopping

Hope emerges

Dr. Robert Mann

In the cold
From the dark
Emerged a light
A calming warmth
A radiant Hope.

Hope that stirs
That challenges
That compels and consumes.
Hope that fulfills
And summons Dreams.

Dreams that are spoken
And Believed,
Dreams from the past
And for the future
Dreams that shed Tears

Tears that unite
Tears unexplained
Yet understood
Tears that reflect freedom
And encourage hope

Hope that emerges
On this day
From these steps
In this cold
For Our posterity

Primary colors

Michelle L. Wardlow

there's the smell
of life in the middle of february
that eludes my wandering eyes
ice turns to water
feeds the little ones'
emerging energies
an eventual reflection
of all the primary colors
and then the sloughing
of their surfaces
and we're left
with the essence of the thing
and the swelling
of our souls

Wilmington, delaware

Alexa Mergen

This was the final stop before freedom
where Tubman led more than seventy
people from pain to promise on a night path
of nooks, songs and constellations. Now beacons
dot bridges so pilots know to look up from horizon.
Sky's gray as birds' wings. The air recalls through swaying
leaves, by the wind lifting a lock of hair or hat brim, that
escape, then rescue, are breath that keep us living.

Dream revisited

Erica Reckamp

we had hope
a vague understanding
of what makes a good man
a distant dream
that would be enough

we had hope
our children
would not learn
to clench down
on poor excuses

some did not wish this

others
took to carrying rulers and tape measures
slyly tracking the breadth
of smiling lips
the length of relieved sighs
cataloguing promise

we had hope
enough to push forward
and watch for the time

slow tick
after slow tick

a time
when

we know hope

Obama: Is he the sun, *Gwen?

Muhammad Tahir Mallam

(*Gwendolyn Brooks, 1917-2000)

The last time the Sun was here
we could not greet him, could not welcome him
partly because of the intense hammering
of his words, nor could our eyes bear
the sight he wants us to see
so we flopped when we sent him
in a cloud of blood behind the White mountains
behind the reach of our belated lamentations

Since then the pounding has never ceased
and the sight has remained, Maya, a *fetid swamp of our tears*

And now a Sun has risen anew, renewed?
from behind the Black mountains
suffused in a cloud of rainbows
holding promises we dread to bear
for those behind the shadow have long *Klux-ed*
our hopes to *boogaloo* on the lacerated streets of Harlem
or serenade our blues in the backwaters of Chicago.

Yet this Sun refuses to go away
inundating the *caged birds* in our hearts
with another sermon of possibilities never before imagined
Then the *caged birds* stirred, afraid to goof again
so we watched, we prayed apprehensive of the intent
as we reach out for the stretched hands across the divide
in a fraternity warmed by the Sun to sprout
the true words of Love.

The agitated *caged birds* in our hearts
sing the song of an audacious hope,
so we hope and believe in the Dreams

long foretold of the sway of our Sun
borne by the compassed Winds.

Let's cut short the celebration
for the new journey is longer,
more treacherous

Though no darkness remains in my cell
but the glare from the Sun on our hands
ain't no less dazzling.

This bombou drum!

Abdul-Rasheed Na'Allah

Flutes, drums, guitars
Variance in sounds
As variance in the rainbows
    of our day
Yet, fixed in the firmness
Of this Bambou.
Obama's dance today
Is fixed in the theatre I saw
In the Old Capitol.

Fixed-gazed, the Parrot's frenzy at home:
Will I sit spellbound on this
CNN coverage, or run out
To the Capitol holding my children!
The words I hear have
Frozen my legs; snow frozen.
Only the warmth of
this speech spurs
the eyes, transfixed on
CNN, not the plead,
a child's plead to her father:
Je ka lo, baba! Let's go to the Capitol and
Be one with the eager crowd in the Lincoln city.

The Old Capitol that day
Was reborn
This is the magical man previously predicted by Lincoln.

That faithful day
Four African children on their father's shoulders
Witnesses to the momentum
A fate sealed in Obama president
All held hands, on the declaration day:

Children and adults
Whites and Blacks
Fixed in a belief
In Abraham Lincoln's words,
New dawn once again!

The stars are competing
In showering our earth with light
The moon is brighter tonight.
How well will the sun shine tomorrow
The morning shall tell.

II.
What a Difference a Day Makes

November 4, 2008

Carol Lem

A light rain this morning, and now
the sky opens onto fresh earth
as Santa Anas blow through the canyon,

and people line up at churches, homes,
community centers – while crows
peck out stories for tomorrow's headlines.

But for her, this is a special day,
at 106, she will put on her Sunday best –
an Easter hat her husband once gave her

when they moved from Selma to Toledo
and the children to California
where they said the opportunities were.

She will put on stockings and heels
though she can no longer walk, and call
her caregiver to pick her up at 6 a.m. sharp,

"To be the first," she says, "never thought
I'd live to see this day."
And across the horizon, a high wind

is whisking away the clouds, pundits
are at their maps etching their lists –
one red and one blue.

But for her, she remembers only white
and black, her father dashing home
in the storm, grabbing wife and kids,

"Where to now, papa?" and her mother
straggling behind, worried that she didn't
turn off the oil lamp

though she would never see it again,
"Those days were hard, but we licked 'em,"
she smiles wickedly, wincing at the

overhead lights as her caregiver rolls her
up to the machine to show her where
his name is and what hole to punch.

On awakening, November 5, 2008   *Vin Parella*

we dare to hope
when the fog lifts
and the soul feels
itself sharpen
around the edges

when the sighs
rise from the well
immeasurably deep
and reason's voice
proclaims itself awake

when the old woman's
eyes grow wide and
shine with joy
because her life will
end with a song

November 5th, 2008

(Fontana delle Tartarughe, Piazza Matteo, Rome)

Marian Kaplun
Shapiro

On this warm November morning a crowd
of young people, dancing around this fountain,
churn the air with shouts of *Obama.*

Not one of us four bronze tortoises
goes by that name or, for that matter,
by Guglielmo, Pietro or Marianna.

Usually we're just lumped together
as in *look at those tortoises*
climbing up that marble basin!

So what has this Obama to do with us?
Do the stubby feet of *his* forelegs barely grip
the rim of a basin, bubbling spring water

just beyond the stretch of *his* neck and tongue?
Has *he* inched his way up from the ground
and hung on so long he can almost taste

that cold water, almost wash off this crud,
barely smell *motorini* fumes or hear
the splat of *piccioni* shit? In case

we lose our footing or need a gentle push,
four slender bronze youths, perched
on our pedestal, reach up with palms cupped

to boost our straining tails and groping hind legs.
Have these young, cheering voices, like a strong,
gathering of hands, lifted him as high?—

so high on a rim of sun-spangled water
he puffs out his cheeks, fast-blinks his eyes
and, as in our dreams, plops in –a big splash.

January 20th, 2009

James Irving Mann

The gentle breaking of the dawn
That brings a sky of blue
Fills our souls with light and song.

Today we know we all belong
As hand-in-hand we view
The gentle breaking of the dawn.

Here we stand united strong-
Our future bright and new
Fills ours souls with light and song.

With a sight clear and calm
We behold a promised hue-
The gentle breaking of the dawn.

Changing winds will right the wrong
And Hope, fresh as morning dew
Fills our souls with light and song.

Yes, our many trials were long
But Faith helped to see us through-
The gentle breaking of the dawn
Fills our souls with light and song.

January 20, 2009

Laura Read

Michelle is wearing all yellow
except for her bright green gloves—
you can see the Obamas' breath
it's so cold, but the sun is shining,
and it's noon now on the east coast.
Here in the west, in my son's first
grade class, it's 9:00 a.m., the parents'
coats are on, but we're all stopped
for a minute, waiting to hear Barack
take his historic oath. When he puts
his hand on the Bible, Anne Marie
leans over to me, whispers
My parents are getting a divorce.
As Obama solemnly swears, she tells me
where she'll be on which days of the week.
I think of her mother on Mondays
and Tuesdays and Wednesdays, wearing
her fur hats and cateye glasses, driving
her empty minivan, the kind with the doors
that open automatically, dvd player flush
with the roof, tinted windows—sealed
tight as a snow globe. And in the spring,
when Michelle has gone sleeveless,
we'll buy pinwheels for Mindi's youngest
whose cancer is right now secretly
metastasizing in the tunnels of his bones.
But for this moment, the trees wear
their sequined sleeves, the ice
holds its breath.

On the invitation of January 20, 2009

Heidi
Kenyon

Because he has gone
to dinner parties
in squalid apartments
and homes without columns

and we hope for
economic genius

and we hope for
cool under pressure

but what we know is that
this guest
helped clear the table
rolled up his sleeves
squirted aquamarine dish liquid
into a sinkful of hot water
and immersed his hands.

January 21, 2009

Lenore Weiss

I did not go to Washington, D.C. for the inauguration of Barack Obama, but went there to watch the 44th President take his oath of office with my friend of forever who knows an aircraft carrier does not turn at right angles and how to spell out words backwards in the clouds. We knew each other's magic. To move through her kingdom, she fashioned garnets for my eyes, and I, her, a velvet cloak, but even with those charms we were knocked about in the finishing pool of sand and glass, and so here we are, two scarred brown and white russets who grew up in the Bronx near Hunts Point Avenue eating yes-i-canapes predicting that none of the pimps and gang members would trouble the mall unless they wished to rouse the ire of the community, sitting in front of a television set on a morning when any sentence could begin with an infinitive as 5,000 portapotties and millions of people lined Pennsylvania Avenue in freezing January at ground truth, which is more exceptional than the president's proposed stimulus package, his latest appointment, and his acceptance speech, for it is unending love that carries us across the river.

III.
Before and After

Exit poll

Scot Siegel

I had a dream:
sweating bullets
Oakland. 1973

Soul-music-
afro-sheen
Nixon. Panthers

Grandmother
didn't trust blacks
Called them all
shvartzes–

Twenty years
grandma dead
Now I wonder how
she would have cast her

Ballot:
white/black?
something
in-between? –

A burning Bush
said *fear*
is our greatest asset

Waged war
for war's sake
said*:*
    be afraid

Today,
I keep

pinching myself
wanting to believe
grandmother
Lied.

I pinch myself
till I bleed
black blood
of our brothers
black blood
of our sisters:
black-brown-red-
yellow-Jew–

I blot my eyes
with the rest of you

Overcome,
& wet with joy

After the day's events

Carol Lem

(January 20, 2009)

Sleepy and cold, the old woman
wanders into Café 322, where they
have gathered – in small groups, in twos,
or alone.

Some came to eat, others to drink,
but all to sit and stand before the same
TV screen looming over the chatter
until glasses are tapped to quiet down.

Between replays and commentary,
she watches them listening to him –
the lyrical flourishes and punctuated
litany of challenges and sacrifices

calling out to us, we who are accustomed
to our choice wines and sprinkled Parmesan.
But what brings her here?
This speech she heard earlier – or this

mingling with strangers, the smell of
sausages and seafood pasta wafting over
tables of t-shirted kindred wearing
"Hope," "Peace," "Yes We Can," and

"Yes We Did" on their chests?
The old woman declines a chair,
"Are you here alone?" the lady asks,
"Would you like to join us?"

"Thank you, no," she says, "I just came in
for a drink and I'm almost finish."

The air is trancelike above plates floating
over the gold and silver linings

of this day as the man on the screen
dances with his wife from ball to ball
to the same tune we could now –
all sing, "At Last."

The old woman remembers the words
awakening in these worst and best of times:
"my lonely days are over and life
is like a song."

Morning after the election

(November 5, 2008)

Shayla
Hawkins

After the electric night
and the seismic shift of its history
came again the morning:
soft and pink as clematis,
a milk-white mist laced in the firmament

And the sun: quiet and strong,
its ribbons of yellow light
splayed and spilling through the sky
like celestial sutures sent
to bind the ruptures and calamities
of vanished years

The sparrows and the wind:
sailing through the air
without sound or song,
as if in reverence
to the night's monumental turning
and the healing and holiness
that have revealed themselves
as this new day's
radiance and grace

In Mexico once—Inauguration Day, January 20th, 2009

Jeff Towle

near Cabo Corrientes, Jalisco, Mexico
(Watching the Inauguration on Satellite TV with Democrats
Abroad)

We walk into that which we cannot yet see.
Say it plain: that many have died for this day.

Inaugural Poem: "A Praise Song for This Day"
—Elizabeth Alexander

Today, I already like to think
I'll say in years to come,
"In Mexico once, I saw my country
coming home, hovering like a dancer
in the music of its chance
to set things right.

"I loved the handsome solemn man
who took the oath and spoke his words
of calm conviction in the noontide sun
of a cold Washington January day,
and my wife wept for joy, her tears,
as always, the firmest testimony
to goodness I've ever known.

"I heard the poet, her words
taut yet generous with hope,
her praise song to the service
not of soldiers only, but also
laborers, slave and free, work

they gave not with guns
but sweat and strength to build
the roads and rails, to plant and pick
the fruit and beans and cotton,
some never knowing
that this day would come.

"I saw the black preacher
with his weathered face and voice,
his remembered years of strife
and fear (and love, even then)
in Mobile and Montgomery,
this man, this day—giving us
the benediction, praying,
believing that the white man
could finally do what's right.

"In Mexico once, I saw
all of this and more," I'll say—
"on a vine-bannered hillside
full of birds and flowers
by the sky-touched blue Pacific
and all of us, expatriates and visitors,
cheering all the way to Washington."

Yes, I think I'll tell that story
more than once in days
to come.
          And today, that's hope
enough at tropical noontide
in another country, loving
my own country more than ever,
headed home tomorrow to America,
her troubles and her hopes,
her beautiful possibility,
her "Yes, we can..."

Donning the office

(Barack H. Obama)

Marilyn Gehant

Small gestures tell: the tilt of your neck,
stretch of your spine, shift of your shoulders
You anticipate the world stage entrance
to accept the gathering acclaim
and face the faces of a whole people.

Dream weavers strengthen the fibers
of your garment with spirits of cotton
pickers, bus riders and other firsts.
You warm to memories of past labors
that throbbed and ached to bring you here.

You wear the cloak of confidence
armed with intellect and conviction.
No need to dress in defensive mail
to repeat the words of promise
and utter the language of leadership.

Somber as your dark woolen coat
you slip on the office with grace,
remind us that we stand together
each inventive citizen, hard worker
with vote upon vote cast for freedom.

These states rebuff regal array;
thus you begin your term bare headed
with trust already won, a full treasure.
Courage lifts your heart, your voice.
You swear to uphold, that we may endure.

Barack Obama inauguration day
Dike Okoro

(January 20, 2009)

Today we have seen
The cherished eagle descend
From the top
Of the Iroko,
And the sun
Holds a great smile.
Let every frown cease!
There's a great river
Singing the great wings.
Let every fear be released!
A marvel to behold
Waits to take
The oath of office
To rename Lincoln's Land
And invoke
The promise of the ancestors ....
He whose face is as
Popular as water,
He whose place
Is now a space
For history,
Towers on a platform reserved for legends.

Look
To the sky
And you will
See
The beauty
In his stride,
A rainbow
Proclaiming the faith of MLK

And the patience of Mandela.
Look
At the faces
Gathered to bear
Witness to his arrival,
And you will
Note
The significance of hope
When humanity raises
A flag for posterity's protection
And the present's ambition.
Today we have seen
The eagle descend
From the top
Of the Iroko.
Mombasa sings
Its wings,
Indonesia chants
Its strings,
America warms
Its heart
With the proud
Flight now
Evicting hope
Like light
In darkness.
Let every voice rise,
Let every doors open.
Today hope has come
Home, and we
Are here to embrace it
With open arms!

Inauguration

Lauren Camp

We have emerged into the glint
of cold sunlight, calling only one name
from hurricane to quiet field,
from a great gash of red stripes
to a village of people swooping and singing,
building the wings of this universe
out of bending bones of history.

On this day of putting things right,
the day reason smooths into promise,
I am proud of my country,
upthrust with light.

When Senator Feinstein says
United States of America,
each gilded word somersaults off her tongue,
flipping and jumping into the air,
into the big world of thieves and saints,
teasing into the ears of other countries
and returning with their stories.
Listening, I am able to release and forgive;
the *still waters of peace* wash over me.

Yes, we are at the bottom
of the ferris wheel, but finally looking up
into the thick blue sky
with Dr. King on the seat next to us,
touching his strong face toward heaven,
freedom words tumbling dark
and able-bodied from his mouth
like expanding light through clouds
into the ears of his blessed congregation.

And the burning gospel of history
rolls forth from Aretha's throat
becoming a slow dirt of blues, wringing
trust from anthems, her voice
ringing with pride.

We have begun rewriting the future
of the shattered world.
The long slow sound of ancient music
waves through the people
who stream like a banner on the lawn.

Grant Park

George Ellis Tanner

*Never had he seen such crowds

Twice in a lifetime the whirlwind
of separate wars, would, after years,
reach the Windy City, Sandbur's Chicago;
each revealing, "The pulse...the heart of the people"
end both played out in a park

in '68 it was an ill wind in August
whipping its anger and frustration around
a convention; slamming peace officer against
peacenik, knocking peace to its knees, and
there was blood on both sides of Clark St.

outside, democracy took its tornadic twist
yet inside the tempest gave a breath
to a minority proclaiming moral authority
while I, a TV witness, took Pride in both
youth protest and statesman address

But on an election evening in 2008
the wind seemed to sing of the plains
of Kenya and Kansas, a song of something
stirring, heralding a shift in landscape and
with the ease of autumn breeze the CROWD came

they walked in, celebrity and common man
all colors and generations, joined in
celebration; the prism of their tears
profession a poet of hope, and
a prophet of dream-promised change

as if we and the World had reason
to dance for rewarded anticipation

like children in the park, it near dark
joyfully acclaiming at Christmas Eve
the first snowfall of the season

---

* from "The Poet thinks about the Donkey" by Mary Oliver

Unexpectedly

Mahnaz Badihian

Unexpectedly, sun is rising on your shoulders
As you come from a long road of battle
While the blood is flowing from our ears
With the bad news penetrating day by day in our soul
While sorrow caves in on our lips and our chest

Remember we were lost in the darkness of history
While trying to find our way at the "railroad"
Ending in exile

Remember together we read
"The Jungle" and "The Color Purple"

We ran on the seaside to counsel the dead birds
To vitalize our dreams by the hope in your eyes
We knew we can bring the sun close to our doorstep
And count the stars that look at us unexpectedly

When the day breaks we will go to the railroad
To free those slaves that worked hard for our silk dress
And skipped towards freedom to greet you
But the truth is that the sun is rising unexpectedly
On your shoulder and the little dormant plants have started
Climbing everywhere towards the sun on your shoulder

IV.
In Context

Obama moon rising

Paulette Pennington Jones

4 november 2008

wind
summer breeze in november
fall sandaled foot patting
autumn hand waving
moving forward
slow good-bye to midnight
fast hello to dawn
audacity and dreams
here now
illuminating the narrative
lifting up the story
krystals for stars
chasing the diaspora
across the night sky
moon racing rising
voting for the afternoon of yes
night full of fruition
moon racing rising
between the buildings
just left of 1130
michigan avenue lightning
julia sighting
playing with the emotions of
my people
dancing

gerri allen coaxes
us with flowers on her toes
sound smoothing from her
new jazz shocks
doodads rock doris

"they ain't playing"
douglas said
"they really playing"
music falling around
our ears chandeliers shining
catching light the sound
turn that ruby red
state obama blue
in the spirit of alice
ravi's smooth too
riding her wave
in john's ocean
obama town sound

obama universe now
riffing the undergirding
growing into the ancestor's prayer
obama moon rising
in the bowels of slave ships
crossing the atlantic
these are the prayers answered
1903 steps to the Africanized white house blackened
not knowing where or when or who or how,
but praying through the cotton fields,
the assembly lines,
the cold repositories of so-called knowledge,
praying for dawn
seeking the suns the daughters to lead us there
the tune we've been waiting for
finally the obama blue stage
the voice wafting on the wind
true measure of a man
desire
passion
cleanliness

obama playing our fathers' instrument
down jericho roads always challenge
but righteous integrity builds
delivers grace sufficient
the treasure is the look forward toward
obama moon rising

Riding at the back of the bus

Maril Crabtree

(New Orleans, 1958)

My skin blazed white against the dark brown seat.
I had a giddy thought: what if the brown of _their_ skins—
those who sat here for decades—rubbed off?

My friend and I, fourteen, were the only whites
seated in the Colored section while brown-skinned riders
defied the Whites Only sign, sat up front, filled every seat.

The other white folks stood and glared at us. I felt the heat
of their hatred. Home at last, I shucked clothes and showered
to flush that red-hot hate and fear from my skin and bones.

Fifty years later I stand elbow to elbow in a multicolored crowd
holding the giddy hope that this brown-skinned man we've elected
can finish the job, can flush hate and fear from our collective bones.

Presidents' names

Vanessa J. Marfin

Subaru hatchbacks with kayak racks
are likely to sport stickers saying:
Worst. President. Ever.
Name unwritten/ implied

But at the back of the bus
and in scrape-muffler hoopties
the people know:

All those names have
always sounded like
whips cracking
smallpox spreading
bullets breaking brown-skinned backs of
boys running back to the border
Remember?
They found him face down in the sand
facing *away* from the promised land

Meanwhile, at the Capitol Tours ticket kiosk
clinking quarters syncopate
echoes of clinking shackles
The enslaved built these monuments
as far as the eye can oh-say-can-you-see
There?
Beneath the sausage cart wheels?
That's where the
filthy
auction block
stood

But on this bright morning
A grandmother looks out

of White House windows
looks over our bloodplain
where shit-stinking lies fertilize
seeds of the dream
Her ancestors were enslaved
Not   She
          And may her feet go in silk
          And may she fetch not one single cup of coffee
          And may she braid her granddaughters' hair
          tightly
In that same spot
where generous Jefferson reiterated
all men are created equal
then gave the *men* he held deed to one
saturday afternoon of rest after
the tobacco was in

On this bright morning
let the world chant
Let the name echo
on sattelite CNN
from Kabul to Caracas
Let text messages
pound   out
the syllables of this new name

This new name sounds not like
ankle irons
buffalo hides burning
scratch of quills on
bills of lading
This name sounds like
bare palms
on conga skin
Obama-Obama-Obama

And even *if* he doesn't deserve it
we chant like he answers the ghost dance
Believing, in him
something is reborn

They were there

Phyllis Wax

We couldn't see them
but they were there.

They were clustered on
the Capitol steps. Made incarnate
they would have filled the Mall
from the Capitol to the Lincoln Memorial.
We couldn't see them
but they were there.

Rosa Parks, Fannie Lou Hamer
and Martin Luther King,
Medgar Evers, Marian Anderson,
Emmett Till, Malcolm X,
Jackie Robinson, James Chaney,
Andrew Goodman, Michael Schwerner,
Bayard Rustin, Paul Robeson,
Thurgood Marshall, Roy Wilkins,
James Farmer, Mary Church Terrell,
Whitney Young, Mary McLeod Bethune,
A. Philip Randolph, James Baldwin

and all the rest who chewed on daily insult and
swallowed the bitter taste of disrespect,
who were humiliated when they tried to vote
or go to school, when they entered a diner
or wanted to use a bathroom or water fountain,
those who were beaten on back roads
of small Southern towns or terrorized
by flaming crosses in their yards,
those who were knocked down by water cannons
and attacked by police dogs,

even the four young girls killed
when their church was bombed,
and those who were lynched
or burned in their homes,
as well as those whose bones still lie
in swamps or riverbeds.

They were all there
in front of the Capitol,
listening to him
repeating the oath
and every one of them,
with tear-filled eyes,
was smiling.

As we wept

Judith Brice

(I)   1920's

Flaunting white gowns they rode through town,
as we cringed and shivered and wept.
To the church they rode and then back down

with crosses aflame, white hoods, and gowns,
as we huddled, and listened and crept.
Flaunting white gowns they rode through town

bringing bloodhound dogs circling 'round
as we ran, and our clothes got ripped.
To the church they rode and then back down.

Burly men, bosses, could hear our sounds,
when beyond the noose and wall, we leapt.
Flaunting white gowns they rode through town.

At night with torches they'd go to the mound.
True terror; as *we'd* seen fire that swept!
To the church they rode and then back down.

They'd circle our houses and then back around,
as we cringed and shivered and wept.
Flaunting white gowns they rode through town.
To the church they rode and then back down.

(II)   Nov. 4, 2008

We'd been doubtful, cynical, full of fears,
as rapt, we watched, then wept
'till wordless, we burst into song and cheers.

There were months of holding back our tears;
through restless nights we hadn't slept.
We'd been doubtful, cynical, full of fears.

The time had passed, nearly two years—
second by second, the minutes they crept
'till wordless, we burst into song and cheers.

We'd struggled by; our memories sear—
of white gowned men and how we'd wept.
We'd been doubtful, cynical, full of fears

that never would a black man clear
the electors' bias: truly be judged adept—
'till wordless, we burst into song and cheers.

At 11:00 sharp the mandate was clear:
as we rose to dance, then wept.
We'd been doubtful, cynical, full of fears,
'till wordless, we burst into song and cheers.

A life in America

Kathryn Ridall

I.

A rebel in the sixties,
I was out on the streets like
so many others, pecking fiercely
at the seeds of injustice.

We were young and righteous
then, crying out for the napalmed
children of Viet Nam, for the ache
of the two Americas, black and
white, for our mothers crouching
low in our fathers' shadows.

Did I love my country?
I cannot say. We were a murder
of crows, squawking furiously,
blind to the winds of freedom
that lifted our wild shining wings.

II.

Years drifted by and our loud
caws quieted. We passed some
laws, men and women, blacks
and whites now able to enter the
old privileged places together.

Did I love my country?
I cannot say.

I learned about the world,
women murdered for helping

girls to read, their bodies tossed
like trash into ditches; women
hidden behind walls of cloth,
their eyes peering through
slits narrow as knives,

and I grew grateful for the
wide streets where I waged
my own battles, degrees earned,
in my family the first woman
with a career— learning slowly
to stand in no one's shadow.

But America had other streets
with people of darker hue,
guns and gangs on every corner,
places where America's bright
laws shone remotely as stars.

And always she launched her
wars—covert wars and cold wars,
guerilla wars and conventional
wars, bombs raining fire and fear
on a country, innocent after all.

For decades, it was thus:
strands of gratitude and shame
twisting together in my uneasy
heart, the taste of dust, never
far from my mouth.

III.

Inauguration Day 2009,
a new president—of blood
both black and white— places
his hand on the bible where
Lincoln once swore his oath.

For months he has spoken words
so like the ones we shouted out
long ago and a new America
has answered, *Yes, it is time.*

Today he stands tall before us
and a many-colored nation stands
taller, freer from the shackles
of our common shame.
Maybe this leader can level our
uneven streets, curb our high-handed
wars, or maybe not, but today
I do not ask if I love my country.

Today I remember my local park,
snippets of foreign languages
drifting peacefully by like wisps of
milkweed, children from everywhere,
side by side, flying kites with
long swishing tails.

This train: January 20, 2009
Melinda Rice

Life was ebullient
for me as a child,
burbled non-stop
like a bubbler fountain
with its seemingly-endless
offerings.

Trains catered to class
when I was a kid,
pulled Pullman cars
with their Negro porters
and the dining car
with its trim black waiters
in their crisp white jackets,
elegant icons
of servitude.

And the trains ran smoothly
along the tracks,
the tracks
that created
the other side of the tracks.
I went there only once.
My mother took us
to have our picture taken
by a talented Japanese.
We weren't supposed to tell my dad;
it was for his birthday.

We kept those secrets when I was a child,
but not for the surprise.
It was grey that day,

a deep winter kind of dismal,
and I still see it that way
in my mind. It's like an old newsreel
about a war, the image
is always black and white.

But things have changed since I was a child,
the fountains and the trains, and most of us
have color TVs. I was watching mine
today: An elegant black man stepped out on stage
and promised to serve us
in a whole new way.
This train's been a long time comin'.

A pellet gun

E. Baker

Lord, I'm a little girl
And this boy at
my new school just
said to me
If it all gets too much
for you, let me know
and I'll shoot you
with my pellet gun
It is 1968
I am one of five students
integrating a
Southern college
this boy
and I
are enrolled in
and he must be thinking
little of me and
much of himself
to make his
inhumane offer
Today, January 20, 2009,
at 1:40 pm
I remember of all things
that offer
after the 44th prez
of the US takes his oath
a little thrown off by
the justice mixing up
the words
The new leader of the
Free World looks like me

For only the second
time in history a person
I expect now
no other child will
be offered a bullet
by someone who feels
her getting an
education is too
much to handle.

Rite of passage

Molly Bernard

My friend, tears in her eyes, sobbed,
"I wish my mother had lived to see this!"

A modern miracle,
Grounded in another presidency,
Brought The Great Society to fruition
Embodied in this one young man from Hawaii.

Those of us who remember the sit-ins,
The dogs, the clubs, the unmasked hatred,
The fire hoses washing bodies down the streets,
Stand breathless, stunned,
That those sacrifices offered on the Altar of Justice
Found favor with the King of Justice.

"The People, Yes," one poet claimed,
Will rise above oppression, given time.
And this is the time for America
To look at the past and say
"It has passed. Thank God Almighty."

May we hold our past in our collective
Consciousness. May we hold our present
In our collective hearts.
And may we hold our future in our hopes
That our children will see more than we have seen,
Will learn better what we have learned,
Will rise above what remains of injustice,
Of oppression, of fear and hate,
And promise us that Yes, They Can advance,
Through the hope and promise which ground this president,
To an even better Tomorrow.

Obama

Diane Judge

"Obama Takes Iowa"
News and Observer (Raleigh, NC) headline
Friday, January 4, 2008

This mountaintop,
familiar
this Sherpa,
new.
Bred of Father Kenya
and Mother Kansas,
first world man,
third world roots,
American construct.

A very patriotic poem

Jacqueline Kudler

(November 4, 2008)

Hours before the acceptance speech,
in the first hush of a November dusk,
under the flag the size of a subway car
(no question of the outcome here—
they'd stitched this victory together
for the past two years—each of the fifty
stars fashioned out of phone calls,
petition drives, web messages from
David Plouffe), they'd gathered at
Myrtle and Willoughby, a dozen or so
cohorts, not one under eighteen
not one over twenty-five, swarmed up
the banked hopes of Brooklyn's other
Broadway, over the bridge into Delancey
where the ghosts of our grandfathers
abandoned their pushcarts to join
the parade, buoyed forward by
the very promise that had borne them
over oceans to the blessed land
and by the time they'd rounded
the Bowery to drive uptown, their
ranks had bud out into hundreds,
picking up hundreds more at St.
Marks Square, where the NYU kids
had long since scuttled all pretense
of study, and all together descended
on Union Square where hundreds more—
a sample scatter of New York's lost,
along with all the shades still hovering
here, left over from the old May Day

parades—all already assembled under
the watchful eyes of General Washington
to celebrate the stunning incoming news
which, with the last warm blast from
California, was in fact final.

First a cheer—a sustained yell heard
clear across to Hell's Kitchen, then—
and this is the part you'd never figure—
someone starts to sing "The Star-
Spangled Banner—the flag bearers
most likely, but soon everyone's singing
our national anthem, which no sentient
American has sung seriously since
Viet-nam, but they are serious now,
we are all serious—"The Star-Spangled
Banner", whose scales only a Pavarotti
could begin to ascend with ease, but
they are all singing now, off-key,
punching out the beat with fists
and cell-phone cameras held high
above their heads, and if you scan the
faces slowly, you'll find her belting out
each word—the young woman with
the great frame glasses, head thrown
back to the night sky, hand over her
heart in the pledge position, the one
we learned in school when we and our
country were so much younger.

V.
Call to Action

Inaugural poem: draft

Vasiliki Katsarou

(to the president as poet)

the stage is set
the mythmakers assembled
the thirst for pomp
for substance, for elevation

we are one
he says

and the image of the cleft
tree

one growing from many roots

how many see
ourselves thus

(us)

irreparably
halved, schissured

broken

mother and father
torn away

wholeness and integrity
what we seek

all the
halves and the nots,
the neither-nors

poets-in-training
keepers of the word

train our gaze

No more

Ben Nardolilli

We have said yes to so much,
And in our silence
The word was still imagined hovering
Over our closed mouths,
No more, no more,
We shall say no more to pauses
Others can impregnate,
We will stand on the ruins,
Our taxpayer dollars at work,
And demand,
No more, no more,
As loud as we can,
With as many voices at once,
A million saying
No more, no more,
A hundred million screaming
No more, no more,
We have seen others spitting and burning,
We say no more, no more,
We have seen plenty with backs turned,
We say no more, no more,
Against the warlords sheltered
In the shade of domes, kept warm
In baths of blood, and flames of burning reserves,
We cry,
No more, no more,
When the flames are gone,
And the night comes,
We will not flee, we are strong,
Stronger than the night, we tolerate it,
Night has been our lord and shelter,

Yet to the night
We will say no more, no more,
Our throats pricked by those words
Our lungs will breath in and out
Those commands, out will,
We will be in love with silence
No more, no more,
And we will greet the dawn this way too,
No more, no more
Until it agrees to stay
And when it must depart, it takes us too,
Out of the cold palms of night.

Kindness

Hugh Mann

Every spring, a bluebird flies down our chimney,
gets trapped in the flue, and makes a tremendous
racket trying to free itself. But birds cannot fly vertically,
so eventually the little fellow falls into the woodstove,
exhausted and defeated. Then we gently rescue him,
take him outside, and watch him fly away. Like the
bluebird, man is trapped, unable to escape or ascend.
And man is waiting for the gentle hand of kindness
to lift him up.

Sleepless

Erica Reckamp

dreams cut
tumbled from the bed

when does the body
know
there is   no sleep
       no rest

closed eyes
just a moment
blind me
calm me, cover me
warm me

the dreams turn
distorted
the body sinks

heavy

so

heavy

this canon ball
stains the chest
but

up!
peel off the scum of sleep

invigorate
the tireless body

recover breath
as the smoke
rises away

A life

(for Tom Longin)

Kathryn Howd Machan

A man may be a basket
woven with moon
and wave and fragile root,
all colors, few colors,
the sound of blue wind blowing
hard, silence of snow's

first breath. He may
offer a circle of sturdy
promise, place where hands
make real work matter,
sweet grain, an apple's curve.
A man may take his years

and wing a pattern of lake
and word and April sky
around the world he's chosen
to give, the strength of him
in others' good use, taking
shape that lasts and lasts.

A man like me

Cecilia Martínez-Gil

(though i am a woman)

i am here because i am an immigrant, like most of us
children of immigrants,
foreigners in their own land,
foreigners in a strangers' land
until barak obama comes and makes us owners of the *possibleness*
even when as of yet we are tied up,
clanging and clinging threads of reality
seizing and re-weaving our shredded souls
weaving
and weaving in colors,
people like quilts...
and then
surprisingly
we find the door ajar
to look up
to watch out
but to reach in
to hold onto what we may believe that we can actually weave
envisioning hope
grasping hope
healing in hope
presiding hope
immersed in floods of nothing-but-hope
thus, his smile
handsome president indeed
charming smile, yes of course
and open
and enduring
such an enduring smile that without causing pandemia is nevertheless,
contagious,

fearless
and yes, sweet
yes ladies and gentlemen, a president with a sweet smile
yes
swwweeeeet,
but hush hush
do not rush rush
and just shush
for barak obama are words that sound like maternal songs
a mother's lullaby
eternal from its primal resonance
original as a thought, the first one
evolving from the sight of the first lit fire
the sigh of hope
warm trustworthy, warless,
an awaited awakening of unwithered dreams
mmmm hush barak obama mbmbmb ooobbbmmm
or a name like a mother's sonnet
hush
built in the strategy of constrains and pains
and liberated beyond its cautions and precautions
its rimes
its riddles
free within
mmmm mmmbbbb oohmmm
a name of the other that becomes a one
a man like other, like we as others
the one
a one
a two, a three
composing the rhythm of a song
of the people for the people to the people
ahaa yes
from the people

from us
the one(s) from all sides
places
cribs
a song that summons to Imagine, to acknowledge that We are the World
that yes we can
a song like puzzled pieces that had a dream
that have a dream of a future that yet strives to be being
benignly being
to be, propelled without force but with vivacity,
and thus, life has a color in him
and not precisely Technicolor, nor digital, nor Photoshopped
but rather with the color of people as earth, as nature, as Earth
hence, he is because i am
and i am because he is
a president that draws from memories of a life like mine, like
yours
like most of ours
like yours
a president that precedes the natural desire for faith
not by names of gods nor by friends of gods nor by destroying gods
but by the nature of a spontaneous desire for survival
and nor of the fittest (necessarily)
thus too,
hence again
a man like a mother
like you, some of you, most of us
all of us who come from another
from a mother
here and there or not there but there
everywhere
from us the speakers with accents like lilts and songs
with voices as cadences
thus, hush, do not rush,

obama a force of wisdom
thriving knowledge
and faith
obama like a force
not military force
but force of realization
real
from you
and me
and them
yes, like *them* too
like him
and yet he is born from us, these times
and we are his mother
as we tell
hush hush
no rush
just wait
to have
for all of us

Let those who love now*

Linda Ferguson

I want to make you good, hot food,
feed you polenta and vegetables and
biscuits filled with steaming fruit,
to cook for you all morning and afternoon,
to make you valentine-shaped cookies and
pies full of dark red cherries and bubbling
juice. I want to feed you all – husband, children,
neighbor, friend, and the parent with an ailing
child, the grandmother left sitting alone in a
single room, the soldier who came limping
home, and the men and women who were
wounded by him too – come, let me prepare
this feast for you, and I'll invite our president too –
come sit with us and your strong wife whose
brilliance outshines all the candles and
stars and the sun at noon, and your
daughters – those daisies of our dull
November doom –
you have inspired us to share our food, to pass
our stories round the table like baskets full of
warm bread, because of you we will knit
sweaters for our neighbors and give strangers our
new blue shoes – come, we will rally, we will
join hands and sing and work and
gather in gratitude.

---

*Thomas Parnell, Translation of the Pervigilium Veneris, "Let those who love now
who never loved before;/Let those who always loved, now love the more."

VI.
A Man for Everyman

The peasant's wish

Mdika Nick Tembo

I wish you were mine,
I wish you came home, to sit with me
on my soot-infested mat
as I screamed my pain
and misery to you.

But you are mine,
today, there was dew on my cheeks
when I learned you healed age-old schisms
that held back your progress
these past eleven scores.

What you've done, child
gives me hope that I, we, too,
can lean on Hope
that tomorrow will surely come.
But I wish *you* led me home.

Cocktails for Obama

Ellen Bass

Obama, I'm making canapés for you,
spreading cream cheese on triangles
of rye bread, assembling slivers of $40 Nova,
studding them with Italian capers.
I'm making Swedish meatballs, hundreds,
rolling the raw meat between my palms.
And Obama, I'm making cheese balls. I bought
jars of baby olives with sweet pimentos.
I'm wrapping each one in a blanket of dough.
They're lined up on my battered cookie sheets
in such straight rows they could be soldiers.

All week I've been scouring Goodwill for martini glasses.
And the man at the liquor store gave me a discount
when he heard they were for you.
Obama, I live in a tract house, down the street
from Burger King, but today it's looking mighty artsy.
I borrowed my friend's tall butcher block island,
we wheeled it up a plank into Janet's '82 Toyota.
I steadied it in the truckbed while she drove home
and now we have a bar for you, Obama.
Obama, I had a fight with my neighbor.
She didn't want to pay $100
to come to the party since she'd already given
money online. But I wouldn't
let her get away with that—and she
even brought flowers too.

The musician who's going to play Chopin's études
got into a car wreck and has a concussion. I told him
he didn't have to come, Obama.
But he's driving down from Sausalito. He says

lions and tigers couldn't keep him away.
Obama, I saw the photos of you holding those babies. I saw
how you looked at each new face,
curious, considering, as though a real person
was living inside that bundled body,
as though each one were a popcorn-size piece
of the great puzzle of humanity.

I'm chopping the last of the Romas
from the garden, rubbing garlic
on bread, drizzling olive oil—six dozen
bruschettas, each one crowned with a sprig of basil.
Obama, I know you don't have time to read this,
but I'm sure you'd like to know
that I'm sweeping the floor for you and I'm dusting places
that have never before seen a dust rag.

I've pulled my mother's strapless lace cocktail dress
out of the attic and I've shaved my legs.
And Janet has reclaimed the country's flag—bought two
and stuck them in the weedy grass by the mailbox.
Obama, I'm brushing my teeth for you.
Take care of yourself and get enough sleep
and don't forget to eat.

A Nigerian elegy

Ismail Bala

(For Barrack Obama)

We are the mysteries that poet wrote
To see the ugly face of reason
We are anxious
And one poem day our fear
Will change into the wills of warriors

There are words that churn me now
Which come loose when I'm rosy
Do you hear the rhythm of our cry?
That we bear temerity
And are able to speak and sing swift victories

And that we never rouse the devil when it is asleep
Or the hand when it feels so soft
Or the words that peel off silently from tongues?
We dream freedom even in our chain
We dream them in pain

That is why our cry is so lyrical
It makes the sky ponder
There are silent mysteries at play
That only reason will bring out
I too have seen the ghost dancing

And they teach me that
This writing is good
They teach me to right it writerly
With care, and always with love
There is a point there

And there is miracle
In every thing that speaks unheard
The cloud is cool with words
The pen is not a rebel
Sincerity is our lord.

Election

1999
Two years before your birth,
we danced on the North Tower roof,
my brother, his wife, their vows.
The sun struck so bold we laughed,
then covered from it. Leaves gathered
in spins around us, our small halos
of happiness lifting into the light.

2001
At four months, I balance you against my chest,
your hair catching my tears as buildings fell,
fire spread, dust became an ocean of salt and blood.
I rocked you, waiting for the door to open,
for your father to come through,
to feel the press of him, the strength of bone.

2008
Your father and I run to rouse you,
to see this world of faces, flags,
a father taking his daughter's hand,
she, 7, you, 7. Tonight you let me lift you.
Your smile rises; you wake to song.

I find myself saying
I wish they were here to see,
Rosa and Martin, Ella and Anna, Medgar and Clyde,
my grandmothers, Geraldine and Bette,
Tommy, and Tom, turned from hope,
each who chose his own end.

For a moment, I bow.
Words uproot within me, begin to surface,

I hold them up, gangly and teeming with weeds.
They rise, even still, because this is our vigil,
our memory, struck into the heart of my son,
beating against my own.

11pm in New York city
Cristin O'Keefe Aptowicz

Somewhere on the Bowery,
a women ran screaming into the bar,
and the bartender knew what it meant,
yelled *LIVE FEED!* to the guys
working tech in the sound booth.

And somewhere in Times Square,
strangers burst into tears, hug each other
huge TVs wrapped around buildings
exploded with the news: Him.
Our next President. That One.

And somewhere in Harlem,
sleeping toddler were woken up,
babies were lifted into the air,
great grandmothers fanned themselves,
smiling, saying, *I never thought*
I'd live to see this day.

And somewhere in Queens,
I sat on a futon with a defrosting heart,
so sure it wasn't going to happen,
I stayed home. I mean, it couldn't happen,
nothing good, nothing good like this,
every really happens, does it?
And then one day it does.

And somewhere in the Brooklyn,
a DJ dropped "Black President" by Nas
and the whole room roared.

The other brother

Vasiliki Katsarou

(When Obama was elected
Brother asked: *And now you think you're black?*)

Once there were two brothers.

I married one.

The other told me,

I don't think you're pretty at all
but if my brother thinks so...

He dubbed me
ethnic,

other, despite his own
Lithuanian-Italian roots

I wonder
was he reacting

to my interest in my own birth
culture, preserving
my name
maiden

my curls, flaring
eyebrow, pronounced
nose?

Brother, why do you remove
us from your world?

Reconsider your mother,
your words

Reconsider your handpicked
wife and daughter

Today I can hear

my roommate's
Jamaican aunt

ask me:
And which island are you from, dear?

For Obama

Dike Okoro

The future of dreams
Rests in believing!

Your face is
The song of many martyrs
And the sun of many hearts

Your smile is
The entrance many await,
Both those afraid

And those unafraid,
When what seemed unreal
Suddenly becomes real.

On the election of Barack Obama   *Marj Hahne*

My: pronoun of my
ownership, lone
holder of the key, lady of the House
of Me. *My, my*:
what's said when a woman walks by,
skirt high on the thigh,
an articulated sigh or echo
of a man whose disbelieving eyes
speak. My body, my skirt: the me
in meek shall inherit the earth. It's my dirt,
my grave to claim, my name
on the stone, my bone
to pick with my favorite God.
Marjorie: my Greek pearl,
tight-lipped and lucent;
Hahne: my German rooster
crowing past dawn. My time
to wake up, to make my words
matter: I am the one
I have been waiting for.
(No patter. No chatter.)
Got a mo' better world on a platter.

My, my, my: I give this,
my word, in triplicate,
to My President.

VII.
Forging a Future

Pilgrim's Progress

Tolu Ogunlesi

On one side, an army of voluble blackberries,
Translating King into textese; on the other
A Klan of epithet dealers, sitting tauntingly

On electric mules. Stretched out around them,
A United Nations of graves and grave histories, watchful.
Above, frames floating, studded with names

Of members of an all-white dream team, possessors
Of star-spangled genes. A mist, a burst
Of bleak breath, rises, to dispossess a people

Of their dreams. Into this carnival will walk
A newborn, newly stranded
On the shores of this wreck-laden river.

Into this mist that roughly massages memory.
He will not be one of them. Nor one of us.
He will simply be the sepia-toned pilgrim who sailed

In, by dawn's early light, aboard a paper boat
With a smudged name. His companions a straw hat, dust-flecked
Overalls, and a bale of cotton, wounded with tears.

None of these will belong to him. The only things he will own
Will be a funny name, tattooed onto a skinny frame;
The dust on his feet, passport of a pilgrim's progress;

And a blackberry. He will be naked, to be clothed
By all who see or hear of him.
In his open mouth, we shall catch a glimpse of all

The tomorrows that hold their seeds but no longer
Their yellowed Deeds; all the coming days
That hold their breath, but no longer their weary debt.

114

Drums for tomorrow

Jude G. Akudinobi

Bring out the drums,
for those who have gone before,
the living and the unborn.

Bring out the drums,
for the calf with no tails,
for whom providence wards off pestilence.

Bring out the drums,
for the gangly sprout,
with cracks in the concrete as shields,
against the elements.

Bring out the drums,
for the dawn which has,
banished solitary dreams.

It is full moon,
webs peel off walls,
dilettantes reel off polls,
madmen and specialists squint at shadows;
some say for inspiration and idioms,
for the riddles of the moment.

What shall we name footprints
stamped in hardscrabble paths?

Bring out the drums,
for the many rivers to cross,
with currents so very deep.

Bring out the drums,
for it is not quite *Uhuru*, yet...

Beautiful awakening

Leon A. Walker

And when the time came
To inspect the soul of America
All the world
Drew in its breath
Poised in hopefulness
That a beacon might signal
Answering the riddle of her destiny
And upon her hallowed shores
They began standing as one
Though the crossroads summoned
And weary of the storm
They resiliently clasped hands
Generations past and beyond
And as they marched
They carried a single banner
The pennant of their homeland
Hoisted high by the masses
Fixed on new horizons
America was awakened
I heard the cries of her people
Demanding their freedom's birthright
The voice of he who would lead them
Spoke simple words of steely truth
The searing mantra
Echoed throughout the world
"Yes we can"

You have come

Olivia Arieti

Almost a dream
For wrists
Still bleeding
Under chains
Of shame
A vision, perhaps
For broken lips
Still cursing
With rage
At last
You have come
To soothe
Our wounded past
And dignify
The uncertain future
Of a country
Where equality
Has now become
More than a word.

With liberty and justice for all
B.R. Strahan

(Afterthoughts, 9 November, 2008)

Shall we gather at the river,
and now will it truly be *beautiful*?
The old question reverberates
like the tongue of a bell rarely rung.

FIRE! FIRE! in a house made of straw.
The caw of that bird above Poe's threshold
sounds a different note now,
of worlds within worlds turning.

The clockwork grinds past a dangerous hour
into unfathomable futures.

Is Barack the butler?

Venus Jones

Is Barack the butler, she asked?
As he scurried at a graceful pace
in a suit and tie. Prepared plans.
Setting the table for the party.
She inspected the platter and plate
he provided. This is real civil service
with a smile, and sophisticated class.
Serving a full course and benefits
for a health conscious family.
Standing by with a white cloth.
Ready to pour the champagne.
Ready to take out the trash.
Ready to clean the house.

January 20, 2009

Julie E. Bloemeke

Watch the place of his heart
  four chambers, four corners of gold

See the sun reach touch
  these words into shine:

   bold
    willing heart
    selflessness
   grows
   a new era

How not to think, savior, star,
   father, this free world.

How not to think, hold this carefully,
   even light can break.

What but the music?   *Kenneth Salzmann*

"All 1960s and 1970s grads of Kent County high schools are
invited to a musical reunion at the Rehoboth Beach bandstand."

Maybe graying women and balding men are gathering
right now in every improbable town that hugs
a two-digit highway pointing vaguely toward America.

Maybe it's turning out we are unremarkable, after all—
unique and universal, just like all the rest.

Maybe it's nothing but the same comfortable crawl
every generation makes toward first things and well-worn
memories, when they start to notice the obituaries
are piling up higher than anyone ever thought they could.

Or maybe it *is* the music, after all.

What but the music might have orchestrated
forgotten revolutions and unforgettable kisses?
What but the music underscored every presumed
triumph and defeat, drew us into church basements
and into cheap apartments in bad neighborhoods,
ripped down walls, egged us on, played us out?

(Some of us never thought we'd make it this far,
and some of us were right.)

But maybe a soundtrack laid down decades ago
can permeate our souls and chart our lives
until one day we begin to see—long after we've
stopped looking—that astonishing rhythms
really did change the world.

What but the music might have bound us then?
What but the music might bind us again?

Afterword: the prose of the world and the poetry of tears

The root meaning of the word "anthology" is a gathering of flowers. In this book, Abdul-Rasheed Na'Allah has gathered words that have flowered into poems. As we enter the collection, Niyi Osundare presents us with a special bouquet, a poem which has grown out of a word which in its musicality is (perhaps especially to Yoruba ears) itself a poem: "Obama". In a sense — a poetic sense – all the poems that follow are musical flowers growing out of that name-word; Osundare's poem is the fanfare that heralds them in.

However, the poem also gives voice to an anxiety only too incident to the fragility of flowers and the promises of politicians and the music of that name: 'How can its poetry / Survive the prose of politics?' — a thought-provoking opposition, though not a new one. In the Romantic age, Hegel contrasted what he considered the primary poetry of the Greek epics with the more prosaic nature of Roman poetry and general culture; in our own times, the late Mario Cuomo, Governor of New York, used to quip that you campaign in poetry but govern in prose. The opposition consists in linking prose and politics together as a pair associated with the everyday real world, where the everyday is seen as unmusical, low and mundane, even sordid — perhaps in the last resort even lethal; poetry by contrast is not paired with anything in the world and is seen as melodious, beautiful, high, ideal, but, precisely because not linked to politics, frail and vulnerable. Prose is instrumental and gets its hands dirty. Poetry is pure, but of no practical use. All these ways of attributing values to the words "poetry" and "prose" are of course only metaphors and metonyms, and as such "poetic". Prose in itself carries no such values and there is no opposition that is intrinsic to the two media. Notwithstanding that, we habitually make the difference between the two words act as a carrier for the oppositions that make up our culture. So, in conformity with that practice, and in search of an answer to Osundare's question, I ask the reader to bear with me as I now make a lengthy foray into the prose of the world and explore an example of these cultural contradictions at work.

On 5 January 2016, Obama made front-page news in four London newspapers. The news was that the President was making another attempt to extend the law regulating the sale of guns to private citizens (a law first passed through Congress by Lyndon Johnson). To gather public support, Obama televised a meeting at the White House with parents of children killed in one of those school shootings for which the US is notorious. Now the front page of a newspaper is usually devoted to matters of national or international importance, things that concern all its readers. A British newspaper would therefore normally place an item primarily of domestic concern to Americans in the section on foreign affairs somewhere in the inside pages. After all, there was nothing novel about this item; Europeans have long been accustomed to wondering at the attachment American citizens profess for their guns. But that wasn't the story. What made it front-page news was the photo that went with it, for the photo showed that the President was crying. I say "crying", instead of the more respectful "weeping". If the occasion for the tears had been a ceremony, such as a funeral, tears would have been allowable, and would have been dignified by the word "weeping". In Osundare's terms, they would have been seen as poetry rather prose. That they were not so seen is part of a specific political history of tears in the United States, a history very much written in newspaper prose.

During the presidential campaign of 1972, the Democrats had a clear frontrunner in Senator Edmund Muskie, the man they intended to nominate as their candidate to stand against Nixon. That was in February. During the campaign, one of Nixon's aides wrote a newspaper article smearing the character of Muskie's wife. Standing defiantly in the snow outside the office of the newspaper that had run the story, Muskie gave a press-conference to refute the allegations. A photograph in a local newspaper appeared to show tears on his cheeks during his speech, but they may have been only melting snowflakes. Both *Time* magazine and the *The Washington Post* reproduced the photo, reporting without qualification that tears were streaming down his face and that he appeared to break down with emotion. In March, Muskie lost the nomination. This incident, known as the "Muskie moment", has become a reference point in the conduct of electoral campaigns in the States. Forty years later a newspaper article remembered it under the heading, 'There's no crying in presidential politics'. Why not?

The simple answer, the answer in prose is: because "men" don't cry. Women cry, and of course children, but not grown-up men, not men managing public affairs — least of all the Commander-in-Chief, for in that last resort of war feelings of humanity must not be allowed to sway important public decisions. This applies as much to a woman Commander-in-Chief as to a man, and to many countries besides the United States. Irrespective of biology, tears are thus heavily gendered in the prose of this world, which is why I put "men" in quotation marks. In the set of oppositions between prose and poetry, tears are poems and there's no place for them in politics.

This opposition goes back a long way before Hegel, in fact all the way to Plato. To justify his exclusion of poets, especially tragic poets, from the ideal state, Plato has recourse to a syllogistic sequence of propositions. Tragic poems stir up feelings of pity and fear in the audience — they make people cry. Feelings of pity and fear are signs of weakness. Therefore the poets must be expelled. The political context of his argument was democratic imperialism and this may shed a light on why he chose to target the poets. Athens had no standing army and therefore depended on all its adult male citizens to fight its wars as a trained militia. She had recently lost her war against Sparta for the domination of Greece. Plato may be suggesting a reason why the Athenians have lost – they've been shedding too many tears over poetic tragedies, the citizens have become effeminate. His argument may be self-consistent in its logic, but it flies in the face of the empirical record, which can be summarised in a similarly syllogistic form, save for the conclusion. Aeschylus was a tragic poet; Aeschylus was also a citizen-soldier who fought alongside his fellow citizens to repel the invasion of the Persians; and eight years after the Athenian victory at Salamis he wrote a tragedy, *The Persians*, evoking pity for the Persians. President Obama's tears belong with Aeschylus and the poets, and whereas Plato wants a more tough-minded citizen militia, Obama enters the theatre of television to deplore the tragic consequences of arming the citizens, especially in a state that, unlike Athens, has a standing army.

This anthology is also a reply to Plato. It shows that ordinary people refuse to subscribe to the false dichotomy of heart and head, public and private. They believe in and hope for a continuity between the feelings and values they experience in their homes and neighbourhoods as children and adults, men and women, strong and weak – a continuity between those private values and the public structures and values of politics and the state. They believe that the public and the private should be more like bands in a spectrum than opposing zones.

That they hope in this way is demonstrated by the fact that on the occasion of Obama's inauguration they had recourse to poems. For a poem is not just a matter of expressing feelings or asserting beliefs. To become a poem, the feelings and beliefs have to be given form and this itself is a value. The rhythm of dance, the sound of music, the beauty of appearance, the symmetries, concatenations and elegance of logic, the proverbial condensations of experience – these give form to a poem. Form thus integrates the whole human being, heart and mind, body and soul. As an act of integration, a poem corresponds to similar principles in life, in politics. Like poets, politicians attempt to give form to life by passing laws, creating institutions, reaching agreements, and those laws and institutions can share in a poem's attributes of beauty, strength, harmony, elegance and truth to feeling and experience.

The fact that citizens of America, Nigeria and elsewhere had recourse to poetry to express their feelings about Obama's election shows that they recognised in him a chance to give political form to their hopes and values. As a response to the election of an American leader this is without parallel since the election of Kennedy. On that occasion, as far as I know, there was no Abdul-Rasheed Na'Allah to gather up an anthology of poems. However, at least when Kennedy was assassinated a pamphlet was published in Onitsha market which I think testifies, like this anthology, to the desire of ordinary people for a poetry of politics. Its title is *The Life Story & Death of John Kennedy* and there is a brief Preface by a Wilfred Onwuka, who one assumes is also the author. It is written in prose, not verse as such, but after some pages recounting the historical facts of Kennedy's political career, it suddenly breaks into pure fiction – I had almost said "into song" — with a section on 'What President Kennedy said before his Soul left the world.' This is a lamentation over the wrongs of this world and, while still laid out as prose, is clearly inspired by and rhythmically modelled on Christ's tears over Jerusalem in the New Testament (Matthew 23). That New Testament passage itself echoes numerous Old Testament lamentations by the prophets over Jerusalem and the people's misfortunes, and also in the Psalms of David — and the psalms are of course poems, in fact songs. The leader weeps over the sins of his people. He cries. There is no opposition between manliness and tears here. At one point Jesus even compares himself to a mother hen.

Now Kennedy never spoke these Last Words, they are entirely

apocryphal, but poetically they are true, true in the sense of what he meant to people. That is why the writer of the pamphlet moves from prose into poetry. It is not only to express the feelings he has for the dead politician but to give those feelings form, a form that combines contradictions and overcomes oppositions in an act of integration.

So here we have the answer to Osundare's question about the music of Obama's name: 'How can its poetry / Survive the prose of politics?' The answer depends on the citizens themselves. In a democracy, the people can make their state into a poem or, as Hitler did, a ruin. There is no logic, other than a fallacious one, that says a President cannot cry and be an effective statesman. The values are social and personal, not abstract universals. In fact there is good hope for a society in which a President may cry. The music that goes with Obama's name is the very American music of 'Yes, we can'. As Kenneth Salzmann concludes the anthology:

> What but the music might have bound us then?
> What but the music might bind us again?

Tim J. Cribb
Fellow Emeritus
Churchill College, Cambridge University

List of Contributors

Niyi Osundare is an internationally acclaimed poet, scholar and award winner, and has published more than 15 volumes of poetry across the world. Among his awards are the NOMA award, the Commonwealth Prize which he shared with an Australian poet and a honorary doctorate degree of the University of Toulous, France. Formally Head of the English Department at the University of Ibadan, Nigeria, he now teaches literature and criticism at the University of New Orleans, New Orleans, USA.

Omofolabo Ajayi, a professor of theatre and African literature at the University of Kansas is currently visiting the department of Anglais, at the Université Gaston Berger BP 234 Saint-Louis in Senegal.

Mdika Nick Tembo holds a baccalaureate in education from the University of Malawi, Chancellor College. He is an Assistant Lecturer in English Literature and he teaches Black History, Afro-Caribbean Literature and English Literature at the Catholic University of Malawi. He is also visiting Lecturer in Shakespeare at Domasi College of Education an affiliation of the Faculty of Education at Chancellor College. His research interests include: gender and development, culture, politics and governance.

Mr **Oritseweyinmi Oghanrandukun Olomu** (St Ifa), Secretary General, Niger Delta Literary Society For Peace And Development.

Megan Webster is a teacher, author, and a freelance editor and translator. Her coauthored texts in English as a Second Language include the So To Speak Listening, Speaking and Pronunciation series. Her third chapbook Bipolar Expres s was published by Finishing Line Press in 2006 after winning the 2004 San Diego Book Award for Best Unpublished Poetry Chapbook and ranking finalist in the New Women's Voices Chapbook Competition. Her poems have appeared in numerous journals and anthologies including Connecticut Review, Sunshine/Noir and Poiesis: a journal of the arts & communication.

Indiana Poet Laureate **Norbert Krapf** is Prof. Emeritus of English at Long Island University, where he taught for 34 years and directed the C.W. Post Poetry Center for 18 years. In 2008-9 he published three books, the first two of which were finalists for Best Book of Indiana: The Ripest Moments: A Southern Indiana Childhood; Bloodroot: Indiana Poems; and Sweet Sister Moon, celebrations of women. With jazz pianist-composer Monika Herzig, he released a CD in 2007, Imagine – Indiana in Music and Words. He is the winner of the Lucille Medwick Memorial Award from the Poetry Society of America and was twice Fulbright Professor of American Poetry in Germany, at the Universities of Freiburg (1980-81) and Erlangen-Nuremberg (1988-89). Since 2004 he has lived and written full-time in Indianapolis, where he serves on the board of Etheridge Knight, Inc.

Erica Reckamp is a mother of four residing in the Midwest. She freelances as an editor/ghost writer and leads poetry workshops. She has published poetry in multiple anthologies and magazines. Erica Reckamp served as managing editor for *Elements Literary Magazine*. She thoroughly enjoys mentoring emerging voices.

Dr. **Robert Mann** has been a teacher of mathematics for 15 years and is not a professional poet or writer and probably not properly defined as a poet. However, he was moved by the power and solidarity surrounding the inauguration of President Obama and felt, even through the TV, the magnitude of this historic event.

Michelle L. Wardlow currently resides in Macomb, IL. She received her B.A. in English at Western Illinois University, and is now enrolled in the Graduate College of Liberal Arts and Sciences, pursuing a Post-Bacc Certificate in African American Studies. She came from a modest home, with her mother being a member of the Armed Services. She hopes to be able to use her own experiences in life as a way to lift up those who are downcast for whatever reason, to let them know that there is still hope, and that the show is not yet over!

Alexa Mergen's poems appear in a variety of journals including Kritya, The Redwood Coast Review, and The Sow's Ear Poetry Review. She is the author of a chapbook "We Have Trees" and a book-length manuscript "Teasing Gold." She writes from Sacramento.

Muhammad Tahir Mallam hails from Minna in Niger State, Nigeria. He teaches English literature in the Department of Modern European Languages & Linguistics, Usmanu DanFodiyo University, Sokoto, Nigeria.

Abdul-Rasheed Na'Allah's poetry collections include *Almajiri* (2001) and *Ahmadu Fulani* (2003). He has read his works in public forums such as the Vancouver International Writers Festival and the African Literature Association conferences. He is also author of critical essays and books published around the world. He lived in Springfield, Illinois from December 2000 to December 2008.

Carol Lem teaches creative writing and literature at East Los Angeles College. Her poetry has recently been published in *Blue Arc West: An Anthology of California Poets, Open Windows, Rattle, and The Chrysalis Reader*. Her memoir essay, *Lem's Café 1968*, from her manuscript, *Journey to the Interior*, was recently published in *Embracing Relationships*. Selected readings from *Shadow of the Plum* may be heard from her CD, *Shadow of the Bamboo*, with soundtrack music composed by Masakazu Yoshizawa. About her work, Lem has this to say: "My poetry reflects an interior landscape shaped by the influences on my life: growing up Chinese American, the 1960s, playing the shakuhachi, a Japanese bamboo flute; teaching and writing. The transforming power of poetry creates order out of chaos, acceptance out of grief and loss. Poetry is a redemptive process for her."

Vin Parella was a high school English teacher for forty-two years. In recent years I have begun to experiment with poetry in its various forms. I am not very good, but I am learning very much. Please feel free to use these verses in your anthology, if you deem them worthy of such an inclusion. The honor to me would be tremendous.

Marian Kaplun Shapiro is the author of a professional book, *Second Childhood* (Norton, 1988), a poetry book, *Players In The Dream, Dreamers In The Play* (Plain View Press, 2007) and two chapbooks: *Your Third Wish*, (Finishing Line, 2007); and *The End Of The World, Announced On Wednesday* (Pudding House, 2007). As a Quaker and a psychologist, her poetry often addresses the embedded topics of peace and violence, often by addressing one within the context of the other. A resident of Lexington, she was named Senior Poet Laureate of Massachusetts in 2006 and again in 2008.

James Irving Mann is an English instructor at National College in Charlottesville, VA. His hobbies include writing poetry and designing greeting cards. He is also a member of University Baptist Church (in Charlottesville as well).

Laura Read received her M.F.A. in poetry from Eastern Washington University in 1997, and since then has been writing poetry and teaching writing at Spokane Falls Community College. Her work has been published in a variety of journals, most recently in *The Sow's Ear*, *The Red Rock Review*, *Edgz*, and *Poet Lore*. She has also published an essay, "Emmanuel," in a collection of essays entitled *At Work in Life's Garden*. Laura has been a Pushcart Prize nominee and a finalist in the *Floating Bridge Press* annual chapbook competition.

Heidi Kenyon is the retired co-founder of a cooking school, a former editor at the University of Idaho Press, a member of the Internet Writers' Workshop and Zeugma Poetry Workshop, and the mother of three. She lives in Seattle, Washington. Her work has recently appeared or is forthcoming in Camroc Press Review and cc&d magazine.

Lenore Weiss is an award-winning writer who lives in the Bay Area. Her collections include "Sh'ma Yis'rael" (2007) from Pudding House Publications, "Public and Other Places" (2003), and "Business Plan" (2001). Her work has most recently appeared in *Nimrod International Journal*, *Copper Nickel*, and *Bridges: A Jewish Feminist Journal* as well as anthologized in *Not A Muse: Inner Lives of Women* and *Appleseeds*.

"Exit Poll" first appeared in *The New Verse News*. It was reprinted in *The Portland Alliance*. It also appears in Scot Siegel's chapbook *Untitled Country* (Pudding House Publications, 2009). **Scot Siegel**'s recent books of poetry include *Some Weather* (Plain View Press, 2008) and a chapbook, *Untitled Country* (Pudding House Publications 2009). His poems have recently appeared in *Windfall*, *The Externalist*, *High Desert Journals*, *New Verse News,* and *The Tonopah Review,* among others. Scot serves on the board of The Friends of William Stafford.

Shayla Hawkins has published poetry, interviews, book reviews and essays in, among other publications, Windsor Review, Carolina Quarterly, Yemassee, Poets & Writers Magazine, The Encyclopedia of African American Women Writers, Tongues of the Ocean, Pembroke Magazine and Calabash. Ms. Hawkins won The Caribbean Writer's 2008 Canute A. Brodhurst Prize in Short Fiction. She lives in Detroit, Michigan.

Jeff Towle (1944-2009) was a firm believer in the power of language and poetry to illuminate the heart's longing for justice. A teacher at Cabrillo College in Santra Cruz, California for almost 30 years, he was a strong advocate for social justice and participated in the college's yearly social justice conference. He loved President Obama and was proud to share the inauguration moment with his countrymen in Mexico.

Marilyn Gehant, a midwest native, has been a fund raiser, career coach, and retreat director. Her poetry has been published in Slant, Rockhurst Review, and Illya's Honey. She has received awards for her poetry from Chicago's Poets and Patrons.

Dike Okoro teaches world literature and English Composition at Olive-Harvey College, Chicago. He earned a PhD in English from the University of Wisconsin-Milwaukee and has two MA degrees in Creative Writing and African American Literature from Chicago State University. His publications include Echoes from the Mountain: New and Selected Poems by Mazisi Kunene (2007), Songs for Wonodi: an anthology of poems (2007), and Dance of the Heart: Poems (2007).

Lauren Camp (Santa Fe, New Mexico) is an artist and educator, working in a variety of visual and literary arts. For more than five years, she has hosted and produced a jazz program on KSFR-FM. Recent publication credits include: The Sow's Ear Poetry Review, Sin Fronteras and Hotel Amerika.

George Ellis Tanner is a retired school counselor. His 35 years as an educator were served at the Yates City School and at Spoon River Valley, District #4. He has earned awards in the Carl Sandberg contest, the Oak Hill competition, and the Peoria Senior Olympics.

Mahnaz Badihian (Oba) is a poet and translator whose work has been published into several languages worldwide, including Persian, Turkish, and Malayalam. She attended the Iowa Writer's workshop with a focus on international poetry while practicing as a dentist in Iowa City. Her publications include two volumes of poetry in Persian and a best-selling translation of Pablo Neruda's *Book of Questions* into Persian. Her most recent publication is a critically acclaimed book of original English language poetry, *From Zayandeh Rud to the Mississippi*. She has an awarding winning selection of poetry (XIV Premio Letterario Internazionale Trofeo Penna d'Autore, Tornio) translated into Italian by Cristina Contili and Pirooz Ebrahimi.

Currently she resides in Northern California where she runs an online multilingual literary magazine, MahMag.org in an effort to bring the poetry of the world together. She presented a paper on erotic literature by Iranian women in the Diaspora at the American Comparative Literature Association's 2008 annual conference. She is a MFA candidate in poetry from Pacific University. A selection of her poems translated by Andrés Alfaro into Spanish will be published in 2009. She is currently working on a collection called "Poems of Protest"

As an associate professor of English at Olive-Harvey College one of the City Colleges of Chicago, **Paulette Pennington Jones** teaches literature, writing, and reading. Her academic training is from the University of Illinois and the University of Pittsburgh, and most recently she studied at the University of Chicago.

Paulette Pennington Jones' poetry, short stories, and essays have been published in *City: A Journal of the City Colleges of Chicago, The Journal of Black Studies, Night Comes Softly,* and *To Gwen, With Love,* and *Warpland.* I also wrote checklist *Theatre Quarterly: No. 18 on Amiri Baraka.*

Her writing mirrors her reality—that of an African American woman living on the south side of Chicago, also the reflection of Africans throughout the diaspora, and always the music that we make.

Maril Crabtree grew up in Memphis and New Orleans but now lives in Kansas City. Maril edited four anthologies of poetry and essays published by Adams Media; her chapbook, *Dancing with Elvis,* was published in 2005. A Pushcart Prize nominee, her poetry has appeared in literary magazines such as *Kalliope, The DMQ Review, The Mid-America Poetry Review, Coal City Review, The Same, Flint Hills Review* and *Steam Ticket.*

Vanessa J. Marfin is a poet, teacher, and mother of two. Her poems have been published in Pemmican Press, an on-line journal.

Phyllis Wax is a Pushcart nominated poet. Her work has appeared in many journals and anthologies, including Out of Line, New Verse News, Free Verse, Lilliput Review, Ars Medica and Wisconsin Academy Review. She co-edited the 2002 Wisconsin Poets' Calendar.

Judith Brice is a retired psychiatrist who practiced in Pittsburgh. She has written poetry for close to thirty years, but since retirement, she now is writing poetry full time. She credits much of her inspiration in writing to her work with patients, to her own experiences with illness, to her love for nature and to her strong feelings about the political world which swirls about us. She has attended many writing workshops over the years and since retirement has been taking courses in poetry writing at University of Pittsburgh and at Carlow University. Her work has been published in several newspapers and reviews including the Pittsburgh Post-Gazette, Poesia , and The Lyric among others.

Kathryn Ridall is a poet from the San Francisco Bay Area. She has published in journals such as The Texas Observer, Kalliope, Pearl, and the Chrysalis Reader. Her chapbook *The Way Of Stones* was published recently by Finishing Line Press and she am the editor of the forthcoming anthology *When The Muse Calls; Poems For The Creative Life.*

Melinda Rice was born in Fresno, California in 1949 and spent her early childhood there. At that time, even California had some pretty strong racial boundaries not only between black and white but for other racial groups also. Now 60, Melinda Rice is a former middle school teacher who advised her students that education and good literature were vital keys to achieving open-mindedness. She encouraged her students to read, read, read in hopes of having a better understanding of all people.

E. Baker is auntie to Marlo, 4, and Roan, 1. She spends time in Georgia, where she writes all she is able to on any subjects her mind takes on when illness does not have her preoccupied with it.

Molly Bernard, a native of Washington, Pennsylvania, earned her B.A. in English at Florida State University and her Master's in English from Barry University. She has taught at the elementary, secondary, and college levels and presently teaches English at Cardinal Newman High School in West Palm Beach, Florida. Ms. Bernard has presented academic papers on subjects ranging from Joseph Campbell to Harry Potter, and she also writes both poetry and short stories of several genres, including mysteries, psychological thrillers, ghost stories, and a few which defy classification.

Diane Judge is a member of the Carolina African American Writers' Collective. Her poem, "Because of Emmett Till," was published in the January 2009 issue of *Black Magnolias Literary Journal*.

Jacqueline Kudler lives in Sausalito, California and teaches classes in memoir writing and literature at the College of Marin in Kentfield. She serves as an advisory director on the board of Marin Poetry Center.

Her poems have appeared in numerous reviews, magazines, and anthologies. Her full length poetry collection, *Sacred Precinct,* was published by Sixteen Rivers Press, San Francisco, in 2003. She was awarded the Marin Arts Council Board Award in 2005 for "an exceptional body of work over a period of time," and her "outstanding commitment to the literary arts."

Vasiliki Katsarou is a first-generation Greek-American poet and filmmaker. She graduated magna cum laude from Harvard College and holds an MFA from Boston University. She has written and directed an award-winning 35mm film called *Fruitlands 1843*. A member of the Princeton, NJ-based U.S. 1 Poets' Cooperative, her poems have appeared in *U.S. 1 Worksheets* and *wicked alice*. She recently co-edited the anthology *Eating Her Wedding Dress: A Collection of Clothing Poems*, published by Ragged Sky Press.

Ben Nardolilli is a twenty four year old writer currently living in Arlington, Virginia. My work has appeared in Houston Literary Review, Perigee Magazine, Canopic Jar, Lachryma: Modern Songs of Lament, Baker's Dozen, Thieves Jargon, Farmhouse Magazine, Elimae, Poems Niederngasse, Gold Dust, The Delmarva Review, Underground Voices Magazine, SoMa Literary Review, Heroin Love Songs, Shakespeare's Monkey Revue, Cantaraville, and Perspectives Magazine. In addition I was the poetry editor for West 10th Magazine at NYU and maintain a blog at mirrorsponge.blogspot.com.

Hugh Mann is a physician-poet whose work has been published in the New Zealand Medical Journal, Irish Medical Journal, Canadian Medical Association Journal, and British Medical Journal.

Katharyn Howd Machan was born in Woodbury, Connecticut, in 1952. Her poems have appeared in numerous magazines, anthologies, and textbooks, and in 30 collections, most recently *Belly Words: Poems of*

Dance (Split Oak Press, 2009) and *When She's Asked to Think of Colors* (Palettes & Quills Press, 2009). A professor in the Department of Writing at Ithaca College, in 2002 she was named Tompkins County's first Poet Laureate.

The native of Uruguay, **Cecilia Martínez-Gil** is a poet, writer, journalist and translator, whose works in English and Spanish have been published in Uruguay and the U.S. A graduate of USC with a B.A. in Comparative Literature and Cultural Studies, she is pursuing her Ph.D. at UCLA where she teaches Spanish.

Linda Ferguson is a freelance writer. Her work has been published in *Four and Twenty, Fickle Muses, Saranac Review, Square Lake, Fireweed, Mad Poets Review, The Oregonian,* and *Equal Opportunity Magazine.* She also teaches creative writing to school children.

Mdika Nick Tembo holds a baccalaureate in education from the University of Malawi, Chancellor College. He is an Assistant Lecturer in English Literature and he teaches Black History, Afro-Caribbean Literature and English Literature at the Catholic University of Malawi. He is also visiting Lecturer in Shakespeare at Domasi College of Education an affiliation of the Faculty of Education at Chancellor College. His research interests include: gender and development, culture, politics and governance.

Ellen Bass's poetry books include *The Human Line* (Copper Canyon Press), named a Notable Book of 2007 by the San Francisco Chronicle and *Mules of Love* (BOA, 2002), which won the Lambda Literary Award. Her non-fiction books include *The Courage to Heal* and *Free Your Mind.* She teaches in the MFA program at Pacific University.

Ismail Bala is a lecturer in English at Bayero University, Kano, Nigeria. He has published his poems in many national and international anthologies, journals, newspapers and newsletters in South Africa, United Kingdom, United States of America, Canada, India, Iceland and Latvia among others. He was the former secretary of the Association of Nigerian Authors (ANA) Kano State Branch. Currently, he is the Editor of *ANA Review*: the national journal of the Association of Nigerian Authors.

Julie E. Bloemeke lives in Alpharetta and is the mother of two young children. Her work has appeared in *Pebble Lake Review* and in the anthology *Lavanderia: A Mixed Load of Women, Wash, and Word*. A series of her poems and photographs is forthcoming in issue 4 of *Ouroboros Review*. Her son, Gareth, was born two weeks before Sasha Obama.

Cristin O'Keefe Aptowicz's work has been published or is forthcoming in McSweeney's Internet Tendancies, Barrelhouse, Monkeybicycle, Pank, decomP, Going Down Swinging, and The Other Journal, among others. My latest book, "Words in Your Face: A Guided Tour Through Twenty Years of the New York City Poetry Slam," was published last year by Soft Skull Press.

Marj Hahne considers herself first a teacher, then a poet, having taught poetry writing, high-school mathematics, English-as-a-Second-Language, Business English, and arts and crafts. A freelance editor and writer, she has performed and taught poetry at over 100 venues around the country, as well as been featured on public radio and television programs. Her poems have appeared in literary journals, anthologies, and several art exhibits, and have been incorporated in the work of visual artists and dancers. She has a poetry CD titled notspeak.

Tolu Ogunlesi was born in 1982. He is the author of a collection of poetry, *Listen to the geckos singing from a balcony* (Bewrite Books, 2004) and a novella, *Conquest & Conviviality* (Hodder Education, 2008). In 2007 he was awarded a Dorothy Sargent Rosenberg poetry prize, and in 2008 the Nordic Africa Institute Guest Writer Fellowship. His poetry has been published in *The London Magazine, Sable, Magma, Stanford's Black Arts Quarterly*, and *World Literature Today*, among others. He lives in Lagos, Nigeria.

Jude G. Akudinobi earned his PhD in Cinema-Television (Critical Studies) from the University of Southern California, and teaches in the Department of Black Studies, at the University of California, Santa Barbara. Dr. Akudinobi's interests span the complexities of cultural politics, media and cinematic representations.

Leon A. Walker is a published writer of various forms of creative literature as well as social and political commentary at: tntalk.wordpress.com . He is a former public and private sector business professional and a retired

United States Naval Officer. Mr. Walker is a graduate of Embry-Riddle Aeronautical University in Daytona, Florida and he is a native of Cleveland, Ohio. He currently resides in Northwest Florida.

Olivia Arieti is a high school English teacher who lives in Italy with her family. She had some plays produced and published in the U.S.A. Her poem, *Daily Trains*, was published in "Women In Judaism", Toronto, June 2008, *"Through The Desert"* in the Wanderlust Review, NYC, July 2009, "Deportation" in Poetica Magazine, August 2009.

Bradley R. Strahan taught poetry at Georgetown Univ. for 12 years. He now teaches at Univ. of Texas. Recently he was Fulbright Professor of Poetry & American Culture in the Balkans. For 30 years he has been editor/ publisher of *Visions-International*. He has five books of poetry and over 500 poems published in: *America, Seattle Rev., Confrontation, The Hollins Critic, Soundings East, Poet Lore,* etc.; several anthologies: 2003 Struga poetry Festival anthology, *Blood to Remember*,etc..

Venus Jones becomes one with each enchanting poem she writes. Her messages promote peace, freedom and justice. She's opened for Def Poetry, produced the poetry troupe Multiverse and shared the stage with Tyne Daly and Grammy-nominated poet Nikki Giovanni. She's a three-time Tampa Bay area slam winner and former slam finalist in the Austin International Poetry Festival. Her poetry has been published in the UK's X magazine, Underground Poetz, Artists Embassy International.

Kenneth Salzmann's poetry has appeared in Sow's Ear Poetry Review, Perigee, The Comstock Review, Rattle, Riverine: An Anthology of Hudson Valley Writers (Codhill Press), Beloved On the Earth: 150 Poems of Grief and Gratitude (Holy Cow! Press), and elsewhere.

Simon Gikandi, internationally renowned scholar and author, is Editor, *PMLA* and Robert Schirmer Professor at Princeton University (USA). His books include *Slavery and the Culture of Taste* (2011), *Ngugi wa Thiong'o (2000), Maps of Englishness: writing identity in the culture of colonialism (1996), Writing in limbo: modernism and Caribbean literature* (1992), *Reading Chinua Achebe: language & ideology in fiction (1991), Reading the African novel* (1987), among many others.

Tim Cribb, scholar and critical thinker, is Fellow of Churchill College, Cambridge University, UK. Among his authored books and scholarly articles are "Kaieteur: place of the pharmakos and deconstruction" *Journal of Postcolonial Writing* (2013), *Bloomsbury and British Theatre:The Marlowe Story* (2007), "Travelling through Time: Transformations of Narrative from Early to Late Dickens" in *The Yearbook of English Studies* (1996),"The Unity of *Romeo and Juliet*', *Shakespeare Survey*, 34 (1990) (reprinted in the Macmillan Casebook on *Shakespeare's Early Tragedies* (1990)), among many others.

Kraftgriots

Also in the series (POETRY) *continued*

Seyi Hodonu: *A Tale of Two in Time (Letters to Susan)* (2008)
Ibukun Babarinde: *Running Splash of Rust and Gold* (2008)
Chris Ngozi Nkoro: *Trails of a Distance* (2008)
Tunde Adeniran: *Beyond Finalities* (2008)
Abba Abdulkareem: *A Bard's Balderdash* (2008)
Ifeanyi D. Ogbonnaya: *... And Pigs Shall Become House Cleaners* (2008)
g'ebinyŏ ogbowei: *the town crier's song* (2009)
g'ebinyŏ ogbowei: *song of a dying river* (2009)
Sophia Obi-Apoko: *Floating Snags* (2009)
Akachi Adimora-Ezeigbo: *Heart Songs* (2009), winner, 2009 ANA/Cadbury poetry prize
Hyginus Ekwuazi: *The Monkey's Eyes* (2009)
Seyi Adigun: *Prayer for the Mwalimu* (2009)
Faith A. Brown: *Endless Season* (2009)
B.M. Dzukogi: *Midnight Lamp* (2009)
B.M. Dzukogi: *These Last Tears* (2009)
Chimezie Ezechukwu: *The Nightingale* (2009)
Ummi Kaltume Abdullahi: *Tiny Fingers* (2009)
Ismaila Bala & Ahmed Maiwada (eds.): *Fireflies: An Anthology of New Nigerian Poetry* (2009)
Eugenia Abu: *Don't Look at Me Like That* (2009)
Data Osa Don-Pedro: *You Are Gold and Other Poems* (2009)
Sam Omatseye: *Mandela's Bones and Other Poems* (2009)
Sam Omatseye: *Dear Baby Ramatu* (2009)
C.O. Iyimoga: *Fragments in the Air* (2010)
Bose Ayeni-Tsevende: *Streams* (2010)
Seyi Hodonu: *Songs from My Mother's Heart (2010),* winner ANA/NDDC Gabriel Okara poetry prize, 2010
Akachi Adimora-Ezeigbo: *Waiting for Dawn* (2010)
Hyginus Ekwuazi: *That Other Country* (2010), winner, ANA/Cadbury poetry prize, 2010
Emmanuel Frank-Opigo: *Masks and Facades* (2010)
Tosin Otitoju: *Comrade* (2010)
Arnold Udoka: *Poems Across Borders* (2010)
Arnold Udoka: *The Gods Are So Silent & Other Poems* (2010)
Abubakar Othman: *The Passions of Cupid* (2010)
Okinba Launko: *Dream-Seeker on Divining Chain* (2010)
'kufre ekanem: *the ant eaters* (2010)
McNezer Fasehun: *Ever Had a Dear Sister* (2010)
Baba S. Umar: *A Portrait of My People* (2010)
Gimba Kakanda: *Safari Pants* (2010)
Sam Omatseye: *Lion Wind & Other Poems* (2011)
Ify Omalicha: *Now that Dreams are Born* (2011)
Karo Okokoh: *Souls of a Troubadour* (2011)
Ada Onyebuenyi, Chris Ngozi Nkoro, Ebere Chukwu (eds): *Uto Nka: An Anthology of Literature for Fresh Voices* (2011)

Mabel Osakwe: *Desert Songs of Bloom* (2011)
Pious Okoro: *Vultures of Fortune & Other Poems* (2011)
Godwin Yina: *Clouds of Sorrows* (2011)
Nnimmo Bassey: *I Will Not Dance to Your Beat* (2011)
Denja Abdullahi: *A Thousand Years of Thirst* (2011)
Enoch Ojotisa: *Commoner's Speech* (2011)
Rowland Timi Kpakiama: *Bees and Beetles* (2011)
Niyi Osundare: *Random Blues* (2011)
Lawrence Ogbo Ugwuanyi: *Let Them Not Run* (2011)
Saddiq M. Dzukogi: *Canvas* (2011
Arnold Udoka: *Running with My Rivers* (2011)
Olusanya Bamidele: *Erased Without a Trace* (2011)
Olufolake Jegede: *Treasure Pods* (2012)
Karo Okokoh: *Songs of a Griot* (2012), winner. ANA/NDDC Gabriel Okara poetry prize, 2012
Musa Idris Okpanachi: *From the Margins of Paradise* (2012)
John Martins Agba: *The Fiend and Other Poems* (2012)
Sunnie Ododo: *Broken Pitchers* (2012)
'Kunmi Adeoti: *Epileptic City* (2012)
Ibiwari Ikiriko: *Oily Tears of the Delta* (2012)
Bala Dalhatu: *Moonlights* (2012)
Karo Okokoh: *Manna for the Mind* (2012)
Chika O. Agbo: *The Fury of the Gods* (2012)
Emmanuel C. S. Ojukwu: *Beneath the Sagging Roof* (2012)
Amirikpa Oyigbenu: *Cascades and Flakes* (2012)
Ebi Yeibo: *Shadows of the Setting Sun* (2012)
Chikaoha Agoha: *Shreds of Thunder* (2012)
Mark Okorie: *Terror Verses* (2012)
Clemmy Igwebike-Ossi: *Daisies in the Desert* (2012)
Idris Amali: *Back Again (At the Foothills of Greed)* (2012)
A.N. Akwanya: *Visitant on Tiptoe* (2012)
Akachi Adimora-Ezeigbo: *Dancing Masks* (2013)
Chinazo-Bertrand Okeomah: *Furnace of Passion* (2013)
g'ebinyõ ogbowei: *marsh boy and other poems* (2013)
Ifeoma Chinwuba: *African Romance* (2013)
Remi Raji: *Sea of my Mind* (2013)
Francis Odinya: *Never Cry Again in Babylon* (2013)
Immanuel Unekwuojo Ogu: *Musings of a Pilgrim* (2013)
Khabyr Fasasi: *Tongues of Warning* (2013)
J.C.P. Christopher: *Salient Whispers* (2014)
Paul T. Liam: *Saint Sha'ade and other poems* (2014)
Joy Nwiyi: *Burning Bottom* (2014)
R. Adebayo Lawal: *Melodreams* (2014)
R. Adebayo Lawal: *Music of the Muezzin* (2014)

Idris Amali: *Efeega: War of Ants* (2014)
Samuel Onungwe: *Tantrums of a King* (2014)
Bizuum G. Yadok: *Echoes of the Plateau* (2014)
Abubakar Othman: *Bloodstreams in the Desert* (2014)
rome aboh: *A Torrent of Terror* (2014)
Udenta O. Udenta: *37 Seasons Before the Tornado* (2015)
Magnus Abraham-Dukuma: *Dreams from the Creek* (2015)
Christian Otobotekere: *A Sailor's Son* (2015)
Tanure Ojaide: *The Tale of the Harmattan* (2015)
Festus Okwekwe: *Our Mother is Not a Woman* (2015)
Tunde Adeniran: *Fate and Faith* (2015)
Khabyr Fasasi: *Spells of Solemn Songs* (2015)
Chris Anyokwu: *Naked Truth* (2015)
Zoya Jibodu: *Melodies of Love* (2015)
Tanure Ojaide: *Songs of Myself: Quartet* (2015)

Printed in the United States
By Bookmasters